WELCOME TO MY WORLD. I HAVE AUTISM.

By Kay Forsman

Illustrated by Leslie Pinto

This book is dedicated to Adam Grensing and Ethan Andsager.

Copyright © 2014 Kay Forsman

ISBN 1505367018

No part of this publication may be reproduced, stored in or introduced into a retrieval system, or transmitted, in any form or by any means (electronic, mechanical, photocopying, recording or otherwise), without the prior written permission of the copyright owner, except by a reviewer who may quote brief passages in a review.

Although the author and publisher have made every effort to ensure that the information in this book was correct at press time, the author and publisher do not assume and hereby disclaim any liability to any party for any loss, damage, or disruption caused by errors or omissions, whether such errors or omissions result from negligence, accident, or any other cause.

Autism is a spectrum disorder, which means my brain was made differently from yours and works differently from yours.

Some children with autism are higher-functioning than others.

When you talk to me, it may seem that I am not listening to you.

I may have a blank look on
my face and stare at you.

You may think I am acting rude, but I am not. Some people call this the autism stare.

This is just what some kids with autism do. Please read more and get to know me, and then you can understand me.

If you decide to sing a song,
I may cover my ears and say,
NO SINGING or STOP!

This doesn't mean you don't sing well,
it just means I have a hearing sensitivity.

Some children with autism sometimes do not like to be touched or hugged. This is called sensory defensiveness.

Some children with autism have a very good memory. I have a good memory and can memorize a whole book or a movie.

Sensory Defensiveness

Perseveration Echolalia

By now you can see people with autism have to deal with a lot.

Hearing Sensitivity

Autism Stare

Different Brain

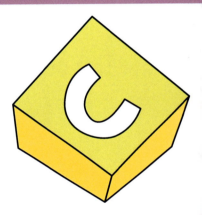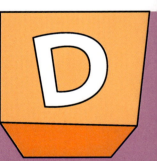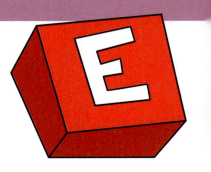

Sometimes you may
see me lining up my toys.
Doing this brings me comfort.
That is called self-calming.

When I am in pain or upset, I may hit myself or someone who is in the room with me. There are many reasons I may do this. One could be I am upset that I cannot tell you I'm upset!

Augmentative and alternative communication may help. This means to use a different way to communicate with me. Like speech devices, eye gestures, pointing, drawing, using pictures and sign language.

If you see me touching certain things in my house over and over again, it is because I have OCD. This means Obsessive-Compulsive Disorder.

Sometimes autistic children laugh or cry for no reason. Sensory overload, diet, imbalances in gut bacteria and overgrowth of yeast, as well as parasites may be the cause.

If you see me rocking back and forth, hand flapping and saying a word over and over again, I am stimming! Stimming is a short word for Stimulatory Behavior.

I could be doing this because I am stressed, angry or upset. It also helps me to calm down.

This behavior is like when you get upset, and you may bite your pencil, bite your nails, play with your hair or tap your foot. You may not know this, but all these things calm you!

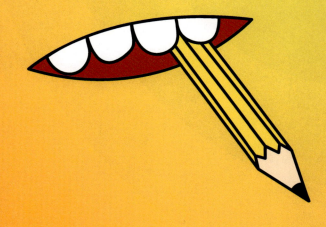

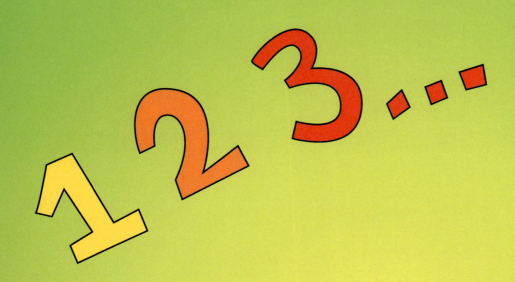

I go to school just like you.
My teachers are called Special
Education teachers.

Children with autism have a hard time making friends.

I like to eat pizza, watch movies and play video games. I also just like to sit in the same room with you for company.

Although there is no medical cure for autism, there is knowledge.

And knowledge is the key to understanding
not only autism but all the
different disabilities people have.

Once you learn about me and understand me,
you will see what a special person I really am.
You might even want to be my friend.

With warmest regards, welcome to my world!
I have Autism.
For more on Autism check
the many Autism websites.

Glossary

Augmentative and Alternative Communication - Using various methods of communication. Examples include sign language, picture and communication boards, and electronic devices.

Autism - A condition characterized in people who have a difficult time communicating and forming relationships with people and in using language.

Autism Perseveration and Echolalia - Perseveration means getting stuck on something, such as a word, phrase, ritual or gesture. Echolalia means repeating what someone says.

Autism Stare - When a person stares into space. Oftentimes, people with autism do this because they are daydreaming of something pleasant or because they are tuning out what may be overwhelming to them.

Different Brain - People with autism have a brain that develops things differently. They have trouble understanding when someone is happy, sad or angry. They may be sensitive to light and noise.

GF, CF, SF Diet - Is a gluten-free, casein-free and soy-free diet.

Hearing Sensitivity - Sensitivity to noise

Obsessive-Compulsive Disorder (OCD) - An anxiety disorder causing people to repeat something over and over again.

Pica - People with pica crave non-food items. Here is a list of some things they may crave: dirt, clay, paint chips, plaster, chalk, cornstarch, laundry starch, baking soda, coffee grounds, cigarette ashes, burnt match heads, cigarette butts, feces, ice, glue, hair, buttons, paper, sand, toothpaste and soap. Pica is a serious health problem.

Sensory Defensiveness/Stimulators Behavior - Difficulty with processing sensory information. The autistic person may react with hand flapping, jumping and head shaking. These are self-stimulatory behaviors.

Stims/Stimming (Self-calming) - Rocking back and forth, squealing, and head banging are a few ways autistic people calm themselves.

Made in the USA
Middletown, DE
15 December 2016